S0-CJN-079

Issues Women Face:

Immoral Past

© 2009
CHRISTIAN WOMANHOOD
507 State Street
Hammond, Indiana 46320
christianwomanhood.org
(219) 932-0711

ISBN: 978-0-9824098-9-3

CREDITS:
Project Manager: Robin Ogle
Page Layout and Design: Linda Stubblefield
Research: Jennifer Bailey
Proofreaders: Rena Fish, Jane Grafton,
Diane Rykhus, Cindy Schaap

All Scripture references used in this booklet
are from the King James Bible.

Printed and Bound in the United States

Acknowledgments

I WOULD BE REMISS IF I did not thank Robin Ogle for her willingness to be in charge of this project. Because of her experience with counseling those who are dealing with an immoral past, I felt Robin was the ideal person to spearhead the gathering of helpful information for this booklet in the "Issues Women Face" series.

May I say thank you to each contributor who took time from a busy schedule to help us with this project. For obvious reasons, we have not revealed the authors. I value each contribution. Each writer saw the big picture of helping others as the Bible says in Galatians 6:2, *"Bear ye one another's burdens...."*

Thank you also to my "unbeatable" team—those to whom I turn when it is time to publish another book—Rena Fish, Jane Grafton, and Linda Stubblefield.

I thank God for each one of you who had a part in making this booklet a reality. Only Heaven will reveal how many people will be helped because of your willingness to share your wisdom.

Mrs. Cindy Schaap

Table of Contents

Preface

ONE OF THE PRIMARY goals of Christian Womanhood Publications is to help women and to help them through the use of Biblical principles. When it comes to helping women, we do not want to leave any stone unturned. Our Christian Womanhood staff has put together a list of delicate issues that women face in the twenty-first century. These issues are being addressed here and will be addressed in our "Issues Women Face" series in the future.

Each volume of this series is a compilation of writings from several godly women who have faced or counseled those who have faced the issue addressed. These are women who know what they are talking about through experience and who have turned to God to be their help. My prayer is that these women will be a help to you as a reader, especially to you who are presently facing these issues.

The "Issues Women Face" series is also being published in an effort to help women who want to help others. There are excellent, Biblical tidbits of helpful advice in each volume. These tidbits will enable those who have **not** faced these issues to be able to help and comfort those who are.

My prayer is that this series will do exactly what it is intended to do—help women. My prayer is that the "Issues Women Face" series will help you in whatever you are facing now. God bless you, and thank you for sharing with us.

Mrs. Cindy Schaap
Senior Editor
Christian Womanhood Publications

From the Perspective
of a Pastor's Wife

by Robin Ogle

> Mrs. Robin Ogle and her husband, Pastor Greg Ogle, both 1993 graduates of Hyles-Anderson College, have been married for 26 years. The Ogles are the parents of Jason, Adam, Anna, Matt, and Elizabeth. Pastor and Mrs. Ogle serve at Calvary Baptist Church in Canton, Illinois. Robin teaches school in the church's Christian school, drives for teenage soul winning, is a member of the WMS, teaches a Sunday school class, and cooks at summer camp. Mrs. Ogle has counseled with many ladies who have dealt with the issue of immorality in their lives.

If there have been tactical errors in your life, maybe the time has come to restructure. From the perspective of a pastor's wife, I would like to encourage you with a few tidbits. My goal is to restore, renew, and refresh: restore your relationship with the Lord and others, renew commitments, and refresh your spirit. My purpose is to further the cause of Christ. With these thoughts in mind, let's go through a few items I sincerely believe can be of assistance.

Restore

It is vital that you restore your relationship with Christ. Take the time to confess each and every sin that comes to mind. I recommend you kneel and confess over I John 1:9 which says, *"If we confess our sins, he is faithful and just to forgive us our sins, and to cleanse us from all unrighteousness."* My reasoning for my recommendation is that you will then have a vivid memory that you Biblically poured out your heart to Jesus. Thank Christ each day for His forgiveness. Doing so will keep the Devil from riding on your shoulder and flashing your sin before your face.

I have found that the closer you are to the Saviour, the more protected you are from slipping into past mistakes. So organize your walk with God.

• Collect your Bible, highlighter, pen, notebook, praise journal, prayer list, and inspirational books. Be sure to keep them handy. Now, **write down** your plan for walking with God, prayer, praise time, and daily devotions.

• Purchase a new Bible. This is a new season in your life, and the Holy Spirit will be teaching you new truths. Jot down these insights in your notebook. The Holy Spirit will also point out special verses. Write these on note cards because they will be your memory verses.

• Read your Bible slowly. You are reading and studying to obtain the mind of Christ, not win the "through-the-Bible-in-a-year" prize. Also, read a chapter of Proverbs every day. You need to rebuild your wisdom database.

• Focus on your prayer list slowly and steadily. Focus on folks in your sphere of influence as well as urgent requests. You can always add more, but at this point it is much more important to be consistent. Pray for growth and for God to place a protective hedge around your life. Ask specifically for direction and yield yourself each morning.

• Take time each day to write down **ten** items in your praise journal. This suggestion might be a chore at first, but you will develop a habit of looking for God's workings in your life all day long. This will keep you close to His side and serve as a reminder that He is with you all of the time.

• Plan to fast one day a week. This has a two-fold effect. One, you will grow closer to God as you fast and pray. Two, you will show your body and feelings that they are **not** in control! You (your spiritual side) will decide when to eat and what to eat. This places your wants and thoughts in subjection—which is where they need to be!

• Be wise when choosing inspirational books. **Please** select books by authors of like faith who exclusively use the King James Bible for references. A must-have is *I Feel Precious to God* by Beverly Hyles. Since the sin of immorality seems to be linked with low self-worth, it is important to seek a Biblical sense of worth. Read a portion of this book every day. Highlight passages that speak to your heart. Write down thoughts in the margin of the book. I also recommend any of the books authored by JoJo Moffitt and *Smile Through the Trial* by Linda Wittig. These books wrap truth in humor. During the times when you feel discouraged or when you tend to "beat yourself up," these books will encourage your heart.

Don't forget to include a few marriage books. Because of the nature of your indiscretion, your marriage or future marriage will be an area that needs fortification. Read *Marriage Is a Commitment* by Dr. Jack Hyles and Cindy Schaap's marriage books (*A Wife's Purpose, A Peaceful Marriage,* and *Lessons Learned From 30 Years of Marriage*). Set the goal of a few pages from one or the other each day.

Another outstanding book is *When Everything Isn't Black or White* by Dr. Jack Schaap. He addresses issues you might be facing. Your life probably has areas that are unique and seem confusing. Dr. Schaap's book will guide you through these issues so you can make sound decisions.

• Oh, a thought on feelings—**don't** trust them! We gals are a fickle bunch. We can feel 20 different ways—and that's before lunch! Dwell on truth. Focus on God's perspective. These are reasons why dwelling in the Bible is so vital.

• Don't forget to converse with Jesus all during the day. Thank Him for your home and family. Ask His counsel about every aspect of your life. Relay your thoughts and feelings to Him often. Let Him into **every** area of your life and don't hold back! He loves you and is grieved when you shut Him out.

• Your personal relationships may have a few foundational cracks. Get ready to use some permanent plaster. Start with the tool of apology. Move on to rebuilding. Instead of gobs of things you **should** do, let's make it easier—**be a blessing.** Whatever it takes, be a blessing with your words, deeds, and thoughts. Have a "be-a-blessing" attitude. This next thought is imperative to apply: don't let others influence how you behave. Expect folks to show their hurt and disappointment in your actions from time to time. Decide now that regardless of others' attitudes, you will be a blessing.

Let me insert a thought on forgiveness. If you have asked a loved one for forgiveness and that person has forgiven you, thank that loved one from time to time. Point out how you admire his Christianity. You may think this would "stir the pot" or bring back past issues. To the contrary, it shows that you realize this person has acted Christlike, **and** it helps thwart the tendency to bring up the past in a negative way.

Renew

Once you have settled your relationship with Christ and others, it is time to recommit. Claim principles by which you will live the rest of your life—**no matter what.** These decisions are based on God's Word—not emotions, situations, issues, or other folks. Some simple principles you may want to embrace are as follows:

1. Be faithful. *"A faithful man shall abound with blessings: but he that maketh haste to be rich shall not be innocent."* (Proverbs 28:20) Be faithful to your chores, your church activities, and your family. The best way to stay faithful is to have a schedule and a calendar. Let them be your conscience.

2. Obey. *"A blessing, if ye obey the commandments of the LORD your God, which I command you this day."* (Deuteronomy 11:27) Decide to obey God's Words, godly counsel, preaching, and your spouse. Refuse to play the situation ethics game; obey regardless.

3. Be separated. *"Wherefore come out from among them, and be* *ye separate, saith the Lord, and touch not the unclean thing; and I will receive you.*" (II Corinthians 6:17) Distance yourself from acquaintances who don't 100 percent promote faithfulness or obedience. Be wary of literature or films which promote ungodly liaisons. Watch out for music which appeals to your sensual nature.

4. Wallow in God's love. "*But God commendeth his love toward us, in that, while we were yet sinners, Christ died for us.*" (Romans 5:8) God loves you! He loves everything about you. Study *love* in the Bible; then pass it along to others. Decide to love even if others seem unlovable.

5. Watch your thought life. "*For as he thinketh in his heart, so is he: Eat and drink, saith he to thee; but his heart is not with thee.*" (Proverbs 23:7) I believe some of the best ways to watch your thought life include following a schedule and keeping your mind busy with uplifting Christian music, teaching CDs, and sermon CDs. When our minds wander, they tend to go into the ditch, not up on the mountaintop. So keep to your schedule and fill your life with the sounds of song and praise!

These five simple principles that I employ are examples to help you get your creative juices running. Find principles that fit your needs and weaknesses. Memorize these Scriptures to keep you on the right path.

Now that you are on the right path, you will probably become a little impatient for your life to be totally pieced back together. "*But if we hope for that we see not, then do we with patience wait for it.*" (Romans 8:25) I encourage you to be patient with your growth and the growth of your relationships. Any builder will tell you it is easier, quicker, and cheaper to build than to rebuild. You are in a rebuilding project. Expect delays. Expect a huge investment of your time, talent, and treasure. Accept the fact that you need to be on God's timetable.

Refresh

This suggestion might seem like a no-brainer activity, but get to know yourself. Develop the talents God has given you. Saying "I don't have any" is not acceptable. You are falling into the pity trap. You are also insinuating that God does not care for you enough to give you any talents. These are both false lines of thinking. You **do** have talents; God **did** give them to you. Write them down. Still struggling? Ask those closest to you what "gold" they see glittering. Then run with it! Look for ways to use your gifts for the cause of Christ. This will keep you from focusing on your faults.

As a final thought, find godly counselors. Your pastor and his wife should be your first choice. They have the spiritual maturity, burden, love for you, and Bible knowledge needed to guide you. They are in the restoration business and will be pleased to help you.

In my heart of hearts, dear lady, I desire for you to face your past, reorganize your thinking, and restore personal relationships. As you read the testimonies which follow, form a written plan that will work for you. Realize that the Lord will help you, your loved ones will support you, and the cloud of witnesses in Heaven will cheer for you. *"Wherefore seeing we also are compassed about with so great a cloud of witnesses, let us lay aside every weight, and the sin which doth so easily beset us, and let us run with patience the race that is set before us."* (Hebrews 12:1)

In a Nutshell:

- Pour out your heart to the Saviour and begin with a clean slate.
- Organize your walk with God.
- Work on personal relationships.
- Nail down what you believe.
- Be patient while you wait on the Lord.
- Get to know the wonderful person you are!
- Seek godly counsel; then follow it.

CHAPTER ONE

God's Grace

"I went by the field of the slothful, and by the vineyard of the man void of understanding; And, lo, it was all grown over with thorns, and nettles had covered the face thereof, and the stone wall thereof was broken down. Then I saw, and considered it well: I looked upon it, and received instruction." (Proverbs 24:30-32)

"Experience is **not** the best teacher; someone else's experience is!" This quote is from the book *To Rejoice Is a Choice* by Dr. Jack Schaap. As you read my testimony, please consider well what I went through. Experience is not always the best teacher. I ask you, as you read, to please learn from what I went through.

I always questioned God about why He placed me with my particular family. My mother and my father never did marry each other. From what I have been told, they lived together for two years, and then my mother returned to her parents' home with me. I have always known who my father is and would even spend time with him and that side of my family.

I felt I was different as a child. I was very shy. I loved classical music and played the piano. I loved to read history. I know this may not sound strange or different to you, but to some of my family members and neighbors, it was. Because I was a young black girl, I wasn't supposed to be interested in those things (or so I was told). It hurt that the people in my life didn't accept me for who I was. I thought that something was wrong with me from an early age. Because I believed something was wrong with me, I also believed that made me less than a person. When I would come home from school, I isolated myself in the house and repeatedly wondered, "God, why don't people just love me for who I am?"

I was a fourth grader when I went with a friend of our family to a Wednesday night Bible study at a Baptist church in Louisiana. I remember holding her hand as I walked the aisle of the church for salvation. Standing in front of everyone, I accepted Jesus as my personal Saviour. I was baptized the next Sunday and was given my first Bible by my grandmother. The church I attended while growing up preached salvation through Jesus Christ, but Bible reading and following God's Word were not emphasized. I cannot remember seeing anyone in my family read a Bible.

The way problems were dealt with in my family usually wasn't very positive. A lot of anger was expressed with loud outbursts. When I was a child, I didn't understand why this was happening. I thought it was my fault that my family was unhappy. I tried really hard to do everything to make them happy by cleaning, cooking, and doing the laundry. Every child should have these responsibilities, but when you are only eight years old, these tasks can be overwhelming.

Some of my family members dealt with their problems with alcohol or drugs. My "drug" of choice was food, and I used food as a way of coping with feeling unloved and useless. I had a serious weight problem, and the neighborhood children and even some of my family members would tease me about my weight. All I could think was "I must not be very lovable, or they would not treat me this way."

As far as my feelings toward God were concerned, I always thought He was just waiting for me to do wrong. I thought God would treat me just like everyone else in my life did. I tried to be really good because I did not want to make God angry. If I did do something wrong, I thought, "Well, I messed up, and God hates me now." Since I never thought I could do anything right, I put myself down constantly. I eventually found a pursuit that made me feel special—music.

I started taking band in the fifth grade, playing the trombone. The next year I started taking piano lessons. Guess what? I was good in music. Nobody cared what I looked like when I played. People noticed me as a person when I played my instruments. Because of the positive attention I received, I practiced often so I could win awards and earn the praise I needed to feel good about myself. The only problem was, I had to keep getting awards to get the praises. What hurt the most is that most of the praise came from people outside of my family. During all this time of excelling in music, I was still attending church and going to Sunday school. However, I still did not see church or God as a way of life.

I left for college in August of 1994. I thought things would get better since I was going away to college. I was accepted into the piano program at Louisiana State University. I felt on top of the world. I had worked hard so I could earn a scholarship. Instead of things getting better when I left home, they got worse. While trying to deal with problems at home, I was having a difficult time keeping up with my course load. At the end of my first semester, I went to my dorm room, sat on the floor, and sobbed because I couldn't handle all the pressure I was under and because I believed myself a failure.

During my junior and senior year of college, I attended a non-denominational church. The pastor talked about how God can help you through anything, but he never did say how to do it God's way. My thoughts still mirrored those I had as a child. "If I don't make God angry, then everything will be okay." Suddenly, my senior year was upon me, and I had never thought about life past college. I decided to continue my education by working on my master's degree in piano. I was accepted into the piano program at the University of Houston in Texas.

By this time I was burned out physically and emotionally. Ever since I was in the eighth grade, my main goal had been to earn a good scholarship to a good university. That goal required an incredible amount of focus and work. By 1998 I couldn't take it anymore. Mentally, I could not handle what was happening at home. I still felt like it was my responsibility to help my family members straighten out their lives. Graduate school was even more stressful than when I was working on my undergraduate degree. I had now replaced my food addiction with an addiction to the Internet. I was still a shy person, so it was easier for me to "talk" to people on the computer. That's how I justified all the time I wasted. I then made some bad decisions concerning whom to date. These unwise decisions just reinforced the idea in my head that I couldn't do anything right. "God still hates me," I thought. "If anything, He probably hates me even more."

Up until that point in my life, I had never been on a date or had a boyfriend. But because I had lost a lot of weight, I thought, "Men might like me now." I had not been with any man intimately. When some men learned this, they didn't want anything to do with me anymore. After this happened several times, I began to think something must be wrong with me. I reasoned from what I saw of the other students around me that I would just have to lower my standards if I were going to "get a man." I wanted something to distract me from all my inner pain. At first the guys I dated were content with kissing and being alone together. After each date though, I felt emptier than I did before the date because of the way I had allowed a man to touch me. I tried to justify the situation by saying, "Well, maybe he wasn't the right one."

By the end of my first semester at the University of Houston, I went into a deep depression. During this time, I started talking to someone on the Internet. He was so sympathetic to my plight of not finding the right man, and I was so hungry for someone to love me and give me attention that I did not care from whom it came. Eventually, I talked to him on the phone, we did meet, and I gave my virginity to this man. As I sit and write this, I still remember the hurt and the shame I felt after we were together. I never heard from him again. What self-esteem I did have at that time was completely gone. I don't know how I continued to function during that time in school. As I look back now, I can see God was trying to work in me, but I could not see it then.

The next man I dated was a Christian, but we didn't act as Christians should when we dated. His mother and father were active in the church. After our relationship ended, his family still invited me to their house for dinner and the holidays. I welcomed the invitations because I did not have many friends. I believe God and Satan were doing battle during this time in my life—not for my soul but for whom my life would glorify. The first time I attended church with this family, I heard about soul winning and the Christian school. One day I was talking with my ex-boyfriend's mother and she said, "God is going to do great things with you." I remember thinking, "I don't see it."

Almost one month after this conversation, I was ready to commit suicide. I felt like God didn't want anything to do with me, and surely no decent man would want me. I felt unsuccessful in dating and college. Because I had been sick that year, I had many leftover prescription drugs, so I mixed all the pills together and got some water. I remember thinking, "Should I take them all at once or one at a time?" I seriously contemplated taking my life, but I could not do it. I broke down and sobbed, wanting the pain to stop. During this time of aloneness, I know God was watching over me, and He stopped me.

In July 2000 I left school to get married. My husband and I moved to the Midwest, back to his roots. I had only known my husband for a short time, and I married him because I thought he was the best I could do and that no one else would want me. I also thought, "Once we are married, everything will be fine." I thought it would be nice to have two incomes and to have someone to love me.

Things did not turn out the way I thought they would. He was not able to hold down a job, and in our turmoil, we both hurt each other terribly. What hurt me the most was his using my weaknesses against me to show how bad a wife I was. I truly thought I deserved to be treated that way. "I am a bad person anyway, so I deserve this."

While I was at work one day, a pastor from one of the Baptist churches invited me to his church. My husband attended a few times, but I do not think he liked it. He never told me I could not go, and he even said, "I think you love God more than you love me." I don't think my answer was right, but I told him, "Yes, I do, and you should love God more than you love me."

After being married for a little over a year, I had to get an order of protection against my husband. As I sat in a bedroom at the house of one of my friends, I knew my life could not continue this way. The years of self-hatred and anger toward my family were still eating away at me. Though I was still attending church, I still wasn't reading my Bible. I finally divorced my husband.

I realized the time had come to make some changes in my life—God's way instead of my way. In November 2001 I finally opened my Bible and began to read. I heard someone say to start reading one chapter of Proverbs every day. When I finally started reading my Bible, I couldn't get enough of His Word. I discovered everything I need to know about finances, relationships, and taking care of myself was in there! The best lesson I learned was how valuable I was to God! The first time I read Matthew 10:31, which says, *"Fear ye not therefore, ye are of more value than many sparrows,"* I started weeping uncontrollably. All my life I just wanted someone to love and accept me for who I was, and Psalm 139:14 says, *"I will praise thee; for I am fearfully and wonderfully made...."* God does have the answers to help us through life! He didn't make a mistake with the family He chose for me. It's no accident this black girl loves J. S. Bach and reading history books!

In February 2004 I began attending an independent, fundamental Baptist church. The preaching that I have received and the Bible reading I have done has helped me to live as God wants me to live. The standards preached in that church are what I have decided to live by.

My testimony is an ongoing one. I have learned from reading the Bible how to deal with my issues. I started a Bible journal, and whatever I was dealing with at the time, I would begin by writing a Bible verse that pertained to that issue. At present I have six Bible journals and periodically read through them. I have noticed I dealt with the same issues over and over but at different times. The following points contain the five ways I have dealt with and still use to deal with my hurts and issues of the past. I pray they will be a help to you.

1. Start by accepting Jesus Christ as *your* personal Saviour. If you haven't figured it out, we all sin. Romans 3:23 says, *"For all have sinned, and come short of the glory of God."* We have to pay a price for that sin: *"For the wages of sin is death; but the gift of God is eternal life through Jesus Christ our Lord."* (Romans 6:23) God loves us so much and does not want us to be separated from Him forever. God sent His Son Jesus to die a terrible death on the Cross to pay for our sin. You have to accept that gift from God. Romans 10:13 says, *"For whosoever shall call upon the name of the Lord shall be saved."* God will not push Himself on you. If you will confess you are a sinner and accept the fact that Jesus paid the price for that sin, He will take you to Heaven when you die. You only have to do this once! God will never discard you; you're His forever. That is not the end of it though. As long as you are alive on this earth, He can use you to further His kingdom.

Many life gurus will give you plans about how to live a successful life. Because I have Jesus Christ in my life, many of the changes I have made have remained because He is the One Who helped me make the changes.

2. Attend a church that bases what it teaches on the Bible. Before I began attending an independent, fundamental Baptist church, I had made several Bible-based decisions about how I was going to begin living my life. I did not realize some churches actually taught about dating standards, finances, and basing one's life on Bible teachings and principles. The best thing about discovering this church was finding people in the church who lived these teachings! My pastor has given me counsel on how to handle family issues.

At first I found it hard to follow what he told me to do, but today I am very happy I did. God has provided great examples of Christians for me to emulate. One couple in my church has "adopted" me into their family. I spend holidays with them, and they have allowed me to share in special occasions in the lives of their children and grandchildren. I have also learned from them about having a godly marriage and how to weather some of life's storms. If it were not for the patience of my wise and godly pastor and the love of the people in my church, I don't know if I would have had the strength to press through many of my storms of life.

3. Spend time alone with Jesus and your Bible. Psalm 46:10 says, *"Be still, and know that I am God...."* In November 2001 I became still, picked up my Bible, and finally made a decision to base my life on the Word of God. I highly recommend you base your dating standards on God's Word before you date. When I was a teenager, I knew that having a physical relationship with a young man was not right. I compromised in this area because I thought intimacy was how to get the love I so craved. I also base my money decisions from what I have read in the Bible. I used to tithe on my net income. One day I read Proverbs 3:9 which says, *"Honour the LORD with thy substance, and with the firstfruits of all thine increase...."* I thought, "I have been giving God what's left after the government and everyone else gets their money." I decided that day to tithe on what I made and to stop giving God the scraps of what was left over.

Ask God to show you what you need to work on to further the plans of His kingdom.

4. Create a plan for living based on the Bible. As I have already mentioned, I have been able to identify some of the issues with which I deal in my life. Do you deal with depression, loneliness, or fear? Write down those issues, and while you read your Bible, purposefully look for verses to help you in these areas. If you experience fear, John 14:1-31 is a great read. Do you feel like you aren't worth anything? Read Psalm 139:17 and 18, and you will realize just how much you are worth. The point is if you do not take the time to read your Bible, you will not find these verses.

Pay attention to the stories of the Bible. The people of the Bible were regular people trying to take care of their families and everyday problems. Learning from their lives is the reason God included them in the Bible. I have often read about Rahab of Jericho, who is generally referred to as a harlot. Still, she straightened out her life and was included in the lineage of Jesus. She was also the great-grandmother of King David. If I hadn't read my Bible, I would not have known what God did in her life. Every time I read about Rahab, I am encouraged that maybe God hasn't given up on me. Read your Bible!

5. Pray. Jesus was in constant contact with God. At times He would go alone to pray. Over the last several years, I have come to understand the need I have to get alone with God. There are times when I cannot wait to get home from work to talk to God. I cannot define *praying* for you. Sometimes when I pray, I scream to God because I feel the load is too much to bear. At times I have just sat silent without saying anything. Go to the Father and ask Him to help you learn from your past. Ask Him to show you how to take something Satan means for evil and make something good come out of it. I have even held back with God sometimes in prayer because everything was so overwhelming. Pour your hurts out to God; He is big enough to handle them.

⌒⌒

I used to think it was an accident that this Southern gal was living in the Midwest. I thought I had messed up God's plan for my life by what I did. Do you know my pastor moved his family to the area nine months before I came? When my preacher tells the story of how he was called to the church I am attending, I think, "Maybe it's not a mistake I'm here. Maybe I didn't mess up God's plan for my life."

I have learned so much and have been able to help other women in our church and even some of my family members with what God has shown me. I have asked God many times, "Why have I had to go through the pain and emotional struggle over the last several years?" Even writing this testimony was difficult for me. I relived each moment I have included in my testimony. I asked God several years ago to help me learn how to deal with my past so I can teach others. I did not think He would take me up on my offer, but He did. I pray my testimony will keep those of you already doing right on His path for you. If you have taken a wrong direction, choose today to get on God's path. It won't always be easy; sometimes it's downright hard. After you have come through, the benefits you reap are so much more rewarding because you followed His way instead of your way.

CHAPTER TWO

Forgive Yourself

Recently I chatted with a sharp gal who had made some poor choices when she was younger. Here is her story.

– Robin Ogle

Susan's* indiscretions began when she was teenager. She felt that in order to be accepted, she needed to be involved in a physical relationship. This pattern of behavior continued for some time. Through a series of miraculous events, Sue received Christ as her Saviour. This gal decided to turn her life around, and she asked God to use her for His glory. God answered this prayer, and today Susan is a pastor's wife of a growing church.

I asked this lady about her thoughts and feelings, how she put the past behind her, and how she stays on the right path. These are some insights Susie had.

Realize that lack of self-worth contributes to poor decisions. Low self-esteem led Sue not to care for her body, appearance, or social skills. Susan's identity was as the popular "party girl," which did indeed bring her the attention she sought. Multiple moves kept her from developing good, solid relationships.

After Susan trusted Jesus, she began to develop a new individuality—one that was centered on Christ. Sue purchased a notebook and a Bible. Each day when she read, she wrote down a truth she could understand. Then Sue prayed for God to help her implement this one truth into her life.

- *"And we know that all things work together for good to them that love God, to them who are the called according to his purpose."* Romans 8:28 was the first verse she studied.

- *"For who hath known the mind of the Lord, that he may instruct him? But we have the mind of Christ."* (I Corinthians 2:16) Little by little she programmed her thought patterns to line up with the Lord's. One day at a time, she learned who she really was. Susie put more focus upon her job, hobbies, and appropriate relationships.

- *"For I will declare mine iniquity; I will be sorry for my sin."* (Psalm 38:18) She needed to ask forgiveness from family members whom she had let down or embarrassed.

- *"I will praise thee; for I am fearfully and wonderfully made: marvellous are thy works; and that my soul knoweth right well."* (Psalm 139:14) Susan began to believe in God's unconditional love and acceptance. If God could love her, then she could love herself.

- *"But God commendeth his love toward us, in that, while we were yet sinners, Christ died for us."* Romans 5:8 became very precious to Sue.

- *"Teach me thy way, O LORD, and lead me in a plain path, because of mine enemies."* (Psalm 27:11) Susan learned that God had a perfect plan for her life. He cared for every aspect of her life. She felt very special and loved.

Today Susan reads her Bible daily and continues to write truths in a notebook. When she battles moments of insecurity, Sue runs to God's Word to reaffirm His love for her. The truth of what God says overrides whatever she happens to be thinking or feeling at the time. Her identity is now firmly placed on Christ. I Corinthians 15:58, *"Therefore, my beloved brethren, be ye stedfast, unmoveable, always abounding in the work of the Lord, forasmuch as ye know that your labour is not in vain in the Lord."*

The wrong companions and activities lead to unfortunate choices. Sue spent many evenings surrounded by friends who participated in inappropriate actions. Viewing questionable movies, reading questionable books, and listening to wrong music led to a rebellious lifestyle and immorality. *"I beseech you therefore, brethren, by the mercies of God, that ye present your bodies a living sacrifice, holy, acceptable unto God, which is your reasonable service. And be not conformed to this world: but be ye transformed by the renewing of your mind, that ye may prove what is that good, and acceptable, and perfect, will of God."* (Romans 12:1, 2)

When Sue was saved, much of her old crowd drifted away. They were not interested in church or the new direction Sue embraced. Though it was difficult at times, Sue realized that she needed to continue traveling on this new path.

There were a few slips, but each time she confessed and then claimed God's promises and helps. *"If we confess our sins, he is faithful and just to forgive us our sins, and to cleanse us from all unrighteousness."* (I John 1:9)

She realized the slips were related to the old pattern of wanting to be liked and accepted. Thus it became all important to make sure that God liked and accepted her over anyone else. These verses or others like them became the foundation of Susan's new life as she separated herself from harmful influences.

- *"When a man's ways please the LORD, he maketh even his enemies to be at peace with him."* (Proverbs 16:7)
- *"Furthermore then we beseech you, brethren, and exhort you by the Lord Jesus, that as ye have received of us how ye ought to walk and to please God, so ye would abound more and more."* (I Thessalonians 4:1)
- *"And whatsoever we ask, we receive of him, because we keep his commandments, and do those things that are pleasing in his sight."* (I John 3:22)
- *"Whether therefore ye eat, or drink, or whatsoever ye do, do all to the glory of God."* (I Corinthians 10:31)

Then some kind ladies at her church began encouraging her to do right. They invited her over for lunch and a ladies' Bible study. No one was judgmental about her dress, her actions, or her indiscretions. Sue believes this acceptance was key in her life. God gave her Christian friends who accepted her on her level. They encouraged growth, but they did not push or demand it. Sue felt very liked and very loved. In retrospect, she admits she did not understand many of the lessons or sermons at church, but she did understand the care extended to her.

Now Susan uses her unique past to minister to ladies from all walks of life. She sincerely tries to accept folks as they are and then nurtures and encourages them in their personal walk with the Lord. *"Judge, not, that ye be not judged."* (Matthew 7:1) *"Judge not, and ye shall not be judged: condemn not, and ye shall not be condemned: forgive, and ye shall be forgiven."* (Luke 6:37) Her insights have helped countless ladies to be restored.

Learn to deal with the times of guilt. Sue felt used and insecure. She hated to see herself in the mirror, and though she was a pretty girl, she felt unattractive. She believed that every trial her family faced was God's judgment on her past behavior. Sue's regrets led to negative thoughts which tore her up inwardly. Unfortunately, Sue tended to take her hurts out on her family. She realized she needed control over her thoughts and emotions. Susan began a Bible study on a woman's spirit. She used 3x5 cards with verses written on them to help in the area of proper attitude.

- *"He that hath no rule over his own spirit is like a city that is broken down, and without walls."* (Proverbs 25:28)
- *"Create in me a clean heart, O God; and renew a right spirit within me."* (Psalm 51:10)
- *"And be renewed in the spirit of your mind."* (Ephesians 4:23)

Susan purposed to replace "stinkin' thinking" with Scripture that encouraged a positive attitude.

Sue still keeps 3x5 cards with encouraging Scriptures printed on them. Daily she reads

- A chapter from the Psalms to dwell on God's love
- A chapter of Proverbs to gain more wisdom

- A chapter of Philippians to keep her joy.

Sue always has a Bible study or two in progress. Next to her bed are a few inspirational books to read before she turns in for the night. Through the years Susie has separated herself from any influence that does not bring her closer to Jesus. Bible memory is very important, and she works on verses weekly. Sue encourages others to drench themselves in Scripture when they are feeling blue, out of control, depressed, or hormonal.

Know the past can be used to help others. Psalm 84:6 says, *"Who passing through the valley of Baca make it a well; the rain also filleth the pools."* Susan shares what she has learned with others. Time each week is set aside to visit and assist those in need. Ladies are encouraged with phone calls, notes, and gifts. Though Susan's past cannot be erased, her sin has been. Sue has come full circle from making poor choices, to making good decisions with Christ, to encouraging others to make better choices.

In a nutshell, Susan's advice is "Forgive yourself; God has." Use the bad for good. Soak yourself with Scripture. Get SUPER involved in a good church. Move forward for Christ and love folks where they are. This is great advice from a lady who has been restored and is being used of God.

*not her real name

Take a Journey With Me

²⁵*And they were both naked, the man and his wife, and were not ashamed.* ¹*Now the serpent was more subtil than any beast of the field which the LORD God had made. And he said unto the woman, Yea, hath God said, Ye shall not eat of every tree of the garden?* ²*And the woman said unto the serpent, We may eat of the fruit of the trees of the garden:* ³*But of the fruit of the tree which is in the midst of the garden, God hath said, Ye shall not eat of it, neither shall ye touch it, lest ye die.* ⁴*And the serpent said unto the woman, Ye shall not surely die:* ⁵*For God doth know that in the day ye eat thereof, then your eyes shall be opened, and ye shall be as gods, knowing good and evil.*

⁶*And when the woman saw that the tree was good for food, and that it was pleasant to the eyes, and a tree to be desired to make one wise, she took of the fruit thereof, and did eat, and gave also unto her husband with her; and he did eat.* ⁷*And the eyes of them both were opened, and they knew that they were naked; and they sewed fig leaves together, and made themselves aprons.* ⁸*And they heard the voice of the LORD God walking in the garden in the cool of the day: and Adam and his wife hid themselves from the presence of the LORD God amongst the trees of the garden.* ⁹*And the LORD God called unto Adam, and said unto him, Where art thou?* ¹⁰*And he said, I heard thy voice in the garden, and I was afraid, because I was naked; and I hid myself.*

¹¹*And he said, Who told thee that thou wast naked? Hast thou eaten of the tree, whereof I commanded thee that thou shouldest not eat?* ¹²*And the man said, The woman whom thou gavest to be with me, she gave me of the tree, and I did eat.* ¹³*And the LORD God said unto the woman, What is this that thou hast done? And the woman said, The serpent beguiled me, and I did eat.* ¹⁴*And the LORD God said unto the serpent,*

Because thou hast done this, thou art cursed above all cattle, and above every beast of the field; upon thy belly shalt thou go, and dust shalt thou eat all the days of thy life: 15*And I will put enmity between thee and the woman, and between thy seed and her seed; it shall bruise thy head, and thou shalt bruise his heel.*

16*Unto the woman he said, I will greatly multiply thy sorrow and thy conception; in sorrow thou shalt bring forth children; and thy desire shall be to thy husband, and he shall rule over thee.* 17*And unto Adam he said, Because thou hast hearkened unto the voice of thy wife, and hast eaten of the tree, of which I commanded thee, saying, Thou shalt not eat of it: cursed is the ground for thy sake; in sorrow shalt thou eat of it all the days of thy life;* 18*Thorns also and thistles shall it bring forth to thee; and thou shalt eat the herb of the field;* 19*In the sweat of thy face shalt thou eat bread, till thou return unto the ground; for out of it wast thou taken: for dust thou art, and unto dust shalt thou return.* 20*And Adam called his wife's name Eve; because she was the mother of all living.*

21*Unto Adam also and to his wife did the* LORD *God make coats of skins, and clothed them.* 22*And the* LORD *God said, Behold, the man is become as one of us, to know good and evil: and now, lest he put forth his hand, and take also of the tree of life, and eat, and live for ever:* 23*Therefore the* LORD *God sent him forth from the garden of Eden, to till the ground from whence he was taken.* 24*So he drove out the man; and he placed at the east of the garden of Eden Cherubims, and a flaming sword which turned every way, to keep the way of the tree of life.*
(Genesis 2:25-3:24)

Come with me on a journey, won't you? You are the most beautiful of all creations, a magnificent culmination of God's work, a true labor of love given to man as a help meet to him from God. God has only one stipulation for you: "Don't eat the fruit from the tree of the knowledge of good and evil." You are given every pleasure imaginable, you have the opportunity to commune with God, and your home is truly breathtaking.

Suddenly a most beautiful, cunning, subtle serpent hisses in your ear. Can you hear him? "Oh, God is withholding something good from you," says the serpent. "Wouldn't you like to be wise like God?"

You think, "Oh, but that fruit looks so good!" Can you picture in your head the moment your mouth sinks into that fruit and its juiciness? I imagine it tastes incredible. No sooner than you bite into it to savor its delicious sensations, something happens that alters the very course of your life forever.

I imagine a series of explosions setting off a full domino effect that begins to take out everything in its path. Death and destruction seep into every corner of your life faster then you can run from it or hide from it. You have brought about the fall of mankind—all because you thought God was withholding something good from you.

Though my name is not Eve, and I was not there when she was beguiled by the Devil, I relate my story to hers in a very eerily similar way. Let me take you by the hand and show you some powerful things I have learned the hard way.

I grew up as an unsaved teenager, desperately searching for love and acceptance. I wanted so badly to fill the God-shaped void in my life with love but did not know where to turn. I was an awkward-looking girl most of my young life, but when I turned 16, suddenly I was being noticed by boys. As a young teenager inundated with music, movies, and the Hollywood mentality, I believed that pre-marital sex was something that looked good. Why should I lose out on experiencing it and wait until marriage? So, I gave myself away before I was married.

The moment I tasted something that was not mine to experience at that time, I saw my life take a drastic turn in the road that would alter my life forever. It seemed as if each time I gave myself away, I would literally give a piece of myself—never to capture it back.

My life took yet another painful twist in my early 20s when I was raped by a boy whom I had once dated. I remember going to the police and telling them through a tear-streaked face what had happened. I also remember the police turning on me and asking why I was so "emotional," why I hadn't fought harder, and what I did to "ask for it"? This incident left a deep scar that would rear its ugly head many times after I married.

Through the wonderful grace of Christ Jesus, I was saved and finally realized that all I had been searching for all those years was realized in a personal relationship with Christ Jesus. Christ literally transformed my life, and only six months after I was saved, I enrolled in Hyles-Anderson College. What an amazing place college was! I truly loved it!

Things went very well, but I was haunted by my past. I feared that God would never allow me to marry a godly man who would accept me and my baggage. In my junior year of college, I met my future husband. I had been doing everything by "the book" and wanted desperately to serve God and follow His guidelines. I graduated with the distinction of being elected to "Who's Who in American Colleges and Universities." I also graduated third highest in grade point average in my class.

I share these accomplishments not as bragging rights but to illustrate how quickly the wrong decisions or a turn from God can alter life forever—no matter who or where you are in life. By all accounts I was doing very well, but my relationship with my future husband grew too close too fast. Instead of finding my security and love from a close walk with the Lord, I tried to find security in the relationship I had with my future husband. We ended up consummating our relationship before we were married—something that has catastrophic effects to this day, yet didn't manifest itself until three to four years later.

Our first year as a married couple was an eye opener for both of us. Just as we were adjusting to each other, to each other's expectations, and to marriage as a whole, I found myself pregnant. Within two years we were new homeowners, new parents, and my husband's job and hours at work had changed drastically. After the birth of our first child, I ended up in a pit of postpartum depression so deep I could not see any light at the end of the tunnel.

Things began to spiral further out of control each year. Many of our problems seemed on the outside to be petty things, but I know that both my husband and I were growing bitter with each other over issues from our past that were affecting our future. I would often deny my husband and push him away from me if he pursued me intimately. If I did allow him to touch me, I was dealing with feelings of rage and anger. My thoughts included "If he really loved me, he would have protected me instead of 'using me' before we were married." I would look at him and view his advances as dirty and his intentions as selfish. The more I rebuffed my husband's advances, the angrier he got. My view of the intimate marital relationship was completely warped and unhealthy, but all the years of wrong thinking and choices looked like a mountain to overcome.

I remember the day when our marriage just died. We both were filled with so much pain and hurt from years of believing the Devil's lies. Our venom and pain were directed at each other, and we became strangers and enemies in our own home. We slept in separate bedrooms, and we rarely if ever spoke to each other. As far as anyone knew, we were a happy family living the American dream.

From the start of our marriage, we had slowly neglected our church attendance. One Sunday our excuse was that we didn't want to put our baby in the nursery. Another Wednesday we were just too tired. Finally weeks out of church became months, and months became years. We visited and attended different churches in the local area, but that quickly stopped too.

My job outside the home brought great satisfaction; I enjoyed getting out and being able to talk to adults and having a break from parenting. My husband and I worked opposite shifts, so I would care for the kids in the daytime, and he would watch them in the evening. The more I worked, the more I began to enjoy the attention and conversation of male and female coworkers.

I was desperately craving attention and love, so I somehow justified the step from male coworker to affair. Again, like Eve, I saw something I wanted and felt that God was depriving me of something good.

- "Why would HE (God) keep love from me?"
- "Why did HE put me in a loveless marriage?"
- "Why did HE allow me to choose and marry the wrong man? I certainly deserve better; in fact, I deserve to be happy, and God is keeping me from happiness."

Can you hear the deafening HISS??? Little did I realize that the same hiss of discontentment and bitterness to which I had fallen victim had crept into my husband's life, and without my knowledge, he had also sought out another outside our marriage. We were in a deep and horrible pit. My husband ended up outside our preacher's door—a church we had not set foot in for several years.

After hearing my husband's plea for help, our pastor agreed to counsel and help us. We both did not realize at that time that the other had been unfaithful. After some hesitation and stubbornness on my part, I finally agreed to accompany my husband to counseling sessions with our pastor. On or around our second or third session, each of our affairs was divulged to each other. I felt as if I had been run over by a bulldozer. Suddenly years of the Devil's lies finally caught up to me, and I saw the ugly, disgusting mess I had created—all from indulging in something that I thought God was withholding from me. My whole life came screeching to a halt, and I panicked. The next day I filed for divorce and set my heart on never turning back. In my eyes our marriage was beyond hope or help; it was dead. The funny thing is that God specializes in the impossible; He has resurrection power!

Without belaboring the details, God began to slowly work in

our marriage. I literally went from telling our pastor that I wanted none of his help to marching into his office and saying that I didn't care what he said or my husband said, but if he would show me what God said about our marriage, I would give it a try for the sake of our children. It was not an overnight transformation; rather, I underwent a slow process of growth that forced me to get to know God and meet Him face to face.

For six months I cried out to God, calling our conversations my "ceiling talks" because for six months I screamed and begged Him to show Himself real to me. I begged Him to show me He loved me. For much of the six months of searching, I felt as if I was just screaming and talking to the ceiling. But something absolutely amazing happened from my daily pestering…God answered in a huge and very real way! In those six months, not only did God answer my prayers, but I began a wonderful journey of getting to know Him, of learning to obey His voice, and of walking by His side. I learned to go to Him with my loneliness and hurt and to trust Him to heal our marriage.

It has been several years since the day our marriage fell off the edge. If I could begin to tell you the blessings upon blessings in our marriage and family, I doubt you would even believe me. God has not only rebuilt a brand-new marriage, but He has also given us the fullest, most wonderful life imaginable! I often look at our children and wonder where they would be if I had chosen to stubbornly pursue my own ideas. I often imagine the depth of pain and loneliness I would be experiencing if I had bought into the lie that God was withholding "Mr. Right" from me instead of my learning to be "Mrs. Right" to my husband—my true "Mr. Right."

Let me be very honest with you when I say that I believe 99 percent of all of our marriage problems were directly due to my stubbornness, disrespect, selfishness and pride, as well as my lack of submitting myself intimately to my husband and my incorrect expectations for my husband to fulfill my every need. I don't want this chapter to be just a testimony with no solutions; this chapter is written for the woman who says, "What do I do to find hope and peace in the face of immorality?"

1. **Read, meditate, and devour the Bible and take God at His Word!** Read, meditate on, and memorize Romans 8:28, which says, *"And we know that all things work together for good to them that love God, to them who are the called according to his purpose."* We must remember that despite all the hurts or mistakes we have made, God is sovereign. He can take the ugliest situations and make them beautiful again IF we trust and turn our will and way over to Him.

Eve made a tragic mistake when she obeyed the voice of the serpent, but God took a horrible situation and made it beautiful by offering His Son, Jesus Christ, as a sacrifice for our sin by dying on the Cross for us. God loves you! If we are saved, there is not condemnation—only hope, **but** we must be willing to do it His way from now on! In my life God has taken all my hurts and mistakes and has used them as a bridge to help other women in similar situations. I am so happy to share my heart with women; I don't cower in shame because I know I have been forgiven. I know I am loved by God, and I know there is GREAT hope in Christ Jesus! Romans 8:1 says, *"There is therefore now no condemnation to them which are in Christ Jesus, who walk not after the flesh, but after the Spirit."* How beautiful! "No condemnation if we walk in the Spirit" means that God will not condemn us, but He does expect us to put away our fleshly appetites and walk in the power of His Spirit! How do we do this?

2. **Daily go to God in prayer and ask Him to fill you with His Holy Spirit's power.** Ask God to show you His will and put aside your own fleshly desires. Ask and beg God to show Himself real to you. Ask Him to show you His profound love for you! Ask Him to show His love very personally and don't give up asking until He answers.

3. **Acknowledge your sin, take responsibility for your part in it, and recognize your actions have hurt God.** Psalm 51 is one

of my favorite and most healing Psalms for many reasons. David wrote this Psalm under the inspiration of the Holy Ghost after he had committed adultery with Bath-sheba. David makes a powerful statement, *"Wash me throughly from mine iniquity, and cleanse me from my sin. For I acknowledge my transgressions: and my sin is ever before me. Against thee, thee only, have I sinned, and done this evil in thy sight...."* (Psalm 51:2-4)

We must recognize that we can never get deliverance from the bondage of adultery because we have been caught and humiliated or because we have been forced to do right. We must get to the place where we recognize that our actions have ultimately hurt God. When we come to the Cross and humble ourselves before God and worship and submit ourselves to Him, then will we start the process of real change. This is key!

4. Confess your sins to God and ask forgiveness. One important point I must mention is that it is so important that we confess our sins and call those sins by name. The words—*adultery* and *fornication*—are ugly and disgusting, and until you confess them and ask for forgiveness from God and from those you have offended, you will not be able to move on to the next step.

I worked with a girl who had just come out of an affair, and for the longest time, she could not say the word *adultery*. She could not admit and look at the ugly thing she had done and the people she had hurt. Her sin had been justified for so long that there was no true remorse and no recognition that her sin had hurt God. When she finally confessed her sin to God and asked forgiveness, I saw her whole marriage and walk with God transform for good.

5. Seek the counsel of your pastor or a strong Biblical counselor and be accountable every day. I can confidently say that without a doubt one of the keys to the wonderful change that took place in my marriage was the seeking out of wisdom from our pastor and pastor's wife. We would regularly meet and counsel with our pastor, and he would continue to point us to Christ and to truth when we could not see hope or a light at the end of the tunnel in our marriage. It is crucial that you find not only a wise and godly counselor to whom you can be accountable, but one who will point you to the only true help there is—Christ.

6. **Shut any doors that could lead down a promiscuous path.** This may seem so simple, but this step is absolutely crucial. Before you can begin to find healing, you must turn away from what is destroying you. The Bible says in II Chronicles 7:14, *"If my people, which are called by my name, shall humble themselves, and pray, and seek my face, and turn from their wicked ways; then will I hear from heaven, and will forgive their sin, and will heal their land."* Please note in the above passage that God will not begin the healing process until His people:

    a.   Acknowledge their sin and humble themselves before Him.

    b.   Pray and seek His face.

    c.   Turn from their wicked ways.

These steps mean making a decision that you were going in one very wrong direction, and now you will purposely walk toward God and His ways. Very practically, this verse means that if you were having an affair with a man at your place of work, you should quit your job and find one where you will never again be in contact with this person. This means to change your phone number, shut down email addresses you may have shared, and throw away any keepsake gifts he has given you. This means finding a person to whom you will be accountable when you are struggling with wanting to call or write or text this person.

7. **Deal with your past**. Close to 90 percent of adultery and other deep-seated marriage issues come from unresolved issues that occurred in a couple's past. I have not yet met a couple struggling with adultery issues who did not indulge in premarital sex. Oftentimes, a couple goes against the counsel of a parent or authority and marries a person when they have been told it may not be

wise. Sometimes the couple hastily marries without a proper courtship because they want to escape their present situation. Some women may have been molested or raped in their past, and these events bring tremendous unresolved baggage to their intimate life. Other women may have incredible fear and insecurity and may have never established a strong walk with God before their wedding. They have made their husband their idol, and when he does not meet their expectations, they bolt. There are many issues a couple may have struggled with that they have brought into their marriage, but it is crucial to identify these issues and deal with them thoroughly with a wise Biblical counselor.

8. Realize that the healing process will not happen overnight. If an affair has taken place, oftentimes it will take as much time to heal the marriage as it took to get into the affair in the first place. This means if the affair lasted six months, it might well take at least that amount of time to "get over" the relationship. It is so hard for the offended person to hear this, but it is normal for the person who had the affair to actually grieve the loss of the other person. Another almost normal process to happen is that usually when the one who offended is finally doing better, the offended party in the marriage will suddenly struggle and find himself more angry and more mistrustful than he has ever been.

It is crucial to be patient with each other and realize that there will be seasons of struggle and flashbacks, anger, and hurt for both the one who was the transgressor and the transgressed. Recognize that victory is gradual not instantaneous.

9. Recognize how your bad decisions will affect your present situations. For the past two years, I have been asked to speak in various forums about promiscuity and the aftereffects of wrong decisions before marriage. Premarital intimacy is like opening a Pandora's Box. This box often looks so beautiful from the outside but once opened can spread great destruction—much like Eve's biting into that delicious forbidden fruit.

The following points are ones that need to be shared with our daughters. It is so important to see where our decisions lead us. When we decide to have intimacy before marriage, some very real consequences will show up about three to seven years after we are married.

A. *A wall of mistrust and disrespect.* Oftentimes, if a girl marries the one with whom she was intimate, she will see her spouse as the enemy who took away her innocence instead of protecting her virtue. Even if the girl initiates intimacy, something deep within her wishes that the boy would have protected her and not taken her purity before its proper time. She will entertain thoughts of "How can I trust or respect him if he was willing to 'use' me before we were married?" This mistrust and disrespect must be dealt with and corrected, or she will proceed to the next step.

B. *The poison of bitterness.* A wife will look at her husband and mistrust and disrespect him for something they both chose to do. Because she does not know what to do with these negative and hurtful feelings, she grows bitter. Bitterness, if left unchecked, will spread like poison throughout her marriage and her walk with God. I guarantee you that a woman who is bitter with her husband is also bitter at God for allowing this to happen in her life.

C. *The sledgehammer of condemnation and guilt.* The decision to be promiscuous before marriage will undoubtedly bring condemnation and guilt. The Devil is masterful at convincing a girl that indulging in intimacy before marriage will not bring any repercussions. No matter what a girl's background, guilt and condemnation almost always follow this decision and seep into the very fabric of a girl's security. Truth must always be used as an antidote to wrong thinking. God's Word says in Romans 8:1, *"There is therefore now no condemnation to them which are in Christ Jesus, who walk not after the flesh, but after the Spirit."*

D. *Cold fish.* A very ironic part of promiscuity and premarital intimacy is that once that woman is married, quite often she will begin to hate the very thought of intimacy in marriage. Especially is this true if proper Biblical thinking of the intimate marriage relationship is not established.

One of my biggest struggles in our marriage was my wrong thinking concerning intimacy within marriage. It has been a huge battle to reestablish right thoughts so that I can act in a loving and warm way to my husband. If there has been any form of pornography included in a woman's past, there is almost a guarantee of a view of intimacy as dirty and improper.

E. *Handcuffs of pressure.* I have spoken to many a woman who says that when she made the decision to engage in premarital intimacy, she felt pressured to marry the one to whom she gave herself. God has designed marriage between one woman and one man for life, so these feelings are God-given. Oftentimes the choice to sleep with a man while dating comes before the commitment that this is God's will for their lives. By placing the cart before the horse, so to speak, much insecurity and wrong foundations in thinking are brought into a marriage. This also leads to point F below.

F. *Seeds of doubt.* God's plan is always perfect. When we sidestep His will and way, we bring along with it a series of destructive thoughts and effects. One of those destructive effects is the sowing of seeds of doubt. The culmination of mistrust, disrespect, pressure, condemnation, and guilt leads to feelings of doubt that begin to grow in a woman's mind. "Maybe I married the wrong man." "Maybe I don't love him." "Maybe this relationship was a mistake all along." These seeds of doubt begin to grow into full-fledged strongholds in our marriage. At this point many a woman makes decisions like divorce, apathy, and adultery that affect their marriage permanently.

G. *Open Doors.* The moment we decide to take something

that is not ours to take, we open doors that can never be completely closed again. The moment Eve bit into the forbidden fruit, she opened a door that brought death and destruction to all of mankind. I don't want to sound like an alarmist, but someone needs to be straight about what happens when we believe the Devil's lie and indulge in something we believe God is holding back from us. We also need to understand why some marriages struggle with the strongholds and sin that they do. Engaging in promiscuity or premarital relationships opens a door into possible marital affairs, divorce, future impurity, and pornography. We invite unclean spirits to set up a stronghold in our lives that can only be overcome by truth.

10. **Finally, realize that the battle is a spiritual battle.** Ephesians 6:12 says, *"For we wrestle not against flesh and blood, but against principalities, against powers, against the rulers of the darkness of this world, against spiritual wickedness in high places."* Your husband is not the enemy; the Devil is, and he uses every possible tool in his arsenal to target marriages. From the beginning of time, if he can make a husband and wife battle against each other, then he knows he can hold captive whole generations of men and women, boys and girls. There is much to say about spiritual warfare, but it is enough to point out that when a marriage is filled with anger, unforgiveness, sexual defrauding, and distraction from an effective relationship with the Word of God, the Devil's fingerprints are all over that marriage. If you are reading this and trying to find true hope for your marriage in the midst of hurt and pain, may I point you to the only weapon that can defeat the Devil's attack, and that is the Sword of Truth which is the Word of God. I encourage you to spend time counteracting the lies with specific Biblical truths. Please remember your spouse is not the enemy; the Devil and his lies are.

11. **Help others who are struggling.** Psalm 51:12, 13 says, *"Restore unto me the joy of thy salvation; and uphold me with thy free spirit. Then will I teach transgressors thy ways; and sinners shall be con-*

verted unto thee." After David's affair with Bath-sheba, he recognized that he had sinned against God and asked forgiveness. Near the end of the Psalm, he asks God to restore his joy so that he can teach and help others who struggle and be a witness unto those who are unsaved.

One of the greatest ways that I have found healing in my marriage is to use my burden and trial as a bridge to help others. My desire is for God to use my testimony to help others. If just one marriage is saved from divorce or one woman kept from leaving her husband and encouraged to seek Christ with all her heart, then it is worth my opening my soul and risking rejection. I believe that God can use even our worst mistakes as mighty tools for His grace. What a great God we serve that He can take a sinner like me and give me a strong marriage, wonderful children, and a life full of joy.

I can honestly say ALL the glory belongs to God! I am just a sinner who has a wonderful, most phenomenal God! Jesus loves and adores you and wants to show Himself strong in your life and in your marriage. Won't you trust Him!? You think your situation is an impossible situation? Let me remind you that our God is a God Who specializes in the impossible! Mark 10:27, *"And Jesus looking upon them saith, With men it is impossible, but not with God: for with God all things are possible."* I challenge you to take your hurts and decide to be a mighty weapon in the hands of God. He loves and adores you and wants to use you and your marriage for His glory!

CHAPTER FOUR

My Story

My story begins as a young Catholic girl who tried not to be bad or get into trouble. My home life was not the best, and I guess you would say that I was a sensitive child. All I wanted to do was to get married and be a wife and a mother. My parents allowed me to date when I was too immature, and by the age of 17, I was expecting a child. I am a perfect example of why parents must protect their children from the world and its influence.

I married at 17½ and had a baby just before my eighteenth birthday. My husband had a good job, but he began to drink and soon brought pornography into our home. This soon destroyed everything we had built. By this time we had two children.

I loved my husband's parents; they filled the need I had for loving parents. My mother-in-law had multiple sclerosis. She was so sweet and never complained about her health. She told me about salvation, but I chose to ignore her words. I was confused by my husband's reaction to life and how his parents lived. I wish now that I had listened to her because I could have saved myself so much grief. When she died, I adopted the philosophy of my father-in-law, who was angry at God. I adopted the thoughts he voiced. "What is the sense of being saved? If someone who had believed in Him and loved Him so much has been stricken in the prime of her life, what good was salvation? It surely didn't keep her from suffering."

Eventually, as my marriage dissolved, I had a one-night stand. This choice started a destructive pattern in my life, and we divorced. For years I went in and out of relationships and marriages. I hid my sin from everyone, but nothing good ever comes from deception. One day out of desperation, I joined Al-anon and began to take responsibility for my life. During this time, I received Christ as my Saviour. I realized that God was guiding me and directing me. He was there all the time; He opened my eyes to the needs in my life.

1. I needed peace. After many years, I started to heal. I had messed up God's perfect will for my life. But He is so merciful. I had prayed for peace, and He gave it to me! My life's verses have become Psalm 119:165, which says, *"Great peace have they which love thy law: and nothing shall offend them."* and Philippians 4:7, which says, *"And the peace of God, which passeth all understanding, shall keep your hearts and minds through Christ Jesus."* A very wise lady put it so well: though I had messed up God's perfect plan, God, in His infinite wisdom and mercy, made a new plan. He can use me to help others in similar situations.

2. I needed forgiveness. I equate myself to the woman at the well. Look at how God used her! In the last few years, the Lord has allowed me to marry a wonderful Christian man who truly loves the Lord and loves me. He prayed for my salvation for years. Because someone loved and cared for me, I have lived the last 16 years attending a Bible-believing church. I have learned to walk with my Lord. I have served Him the best I know how and will continue to do so until the day I die. I am happier than I ever thought possible. Once I learned how to forgive myself for my sins, my life took on new meaning. I could help others as I have always longed to do. Psalm 103:12 states, *"As far as the east is from the west, so far hath he removed our transgressions from us."* Psalm 103:17 says, *"But the mercy of the LORD is from everlasting to everlasting upon them that fear him, and his righteousness unto children's children."*

3. I needed Jesus. Looking back, I know that there was a "hole" in me. I was trying to fill it with a human relationship. Once I found Jesus, the hole in me was filled with the Holy Spirit. Jesus taught me to love myself so I could finally love another.

4. I needed to serve the Lord. I have been able to grow in the

Lord by reading my Bible. I learned how important prayer is and to serve the Lord whenever and wherever I can. Deuteronomy 11:13, 21, *"And it shall come to pass, if ye shall hearken diligently unto my commandments which I command you this day, to love the LORD your God, and to serve him with all your heart and with all your soul.* ²¹*That your days may be multiplied, and the days of your children, in the land which the LORD sware unto your fathers to give them, as the days of heaven upon the earth."* Jesus will bless you and bring you such joy—a joy that comes from a forgiving, merciful, and loving God. You will then learn to forgive yourself as He has forgiven you.

   5.   I needed the Bible. I needed to learn things from a Biblical point of view. II Corinthians 5:17, *"Therefore if any man be in Christ, he is a new creature: old things are passed away; behold, all things are become new."* II Corinthians 10:3, *"For though we walk in the flesh, we do not war after the flesh."* I want to be a new person—one who looks at every situation through God's eyes.

   6.   I needed to keep my heart clean. Remember that every sin has its origin in the heart. Jeremiah 17:9, *"The heart is deceitful above all things, and desperately wicked: who can know it?* Proverbs 4:23, *"Keep thy heart with all diligence; for out of it are the issues of life."* Romans 13:14, *"But put ye on the Lord Jesus Christ, and make not provision for the flesh, to fulfil the lusts thereof."* This is why it is so important to keep your heart clean. Fill your mind and heart with things of the Lord.

   7.   I needed to dwell on my new life in Christ. My time left is precious. I cannot waste time worrying and fretting over the past because then the Devil wins. Instead, I can be giving my time to Jesus and enjoying the joy and blessings that come from serving the Lord and others. I must not ruin the good I can do today by dwelling on the past. I will only revisit the past when doing so can help another. Whenever the ghosts of the past come up, I pray and replace the negative with a positive. I have found that I cannot dwell on the past and pray at the same time, so prayer always works for me!

Today my sin has helped to make me who I am because I overcame it with the help of my God and allowed Him to use me however He wishes. I am at peace!

CHAPTER FIVE

The Adversities of Life

Seemingly, my life has had several beginnings and several endings. I am the oldest of ten children. My unsaved parents divorced when I was six years old. At the time of their divorce, my alcoholic dad was abusing my mother. My mom took care of us the best she knew how. By the time she finally packed us up and left, I had seen some signs of my father's physical abuse.

Thankfully, one summer my mom and stepdad took us to Minnesota to visit my biological father and stepmother. While visiting with an aunt and uncle, I received Christ as my Saviour. That same year, my aunt and uncle led both sets of my parents to Christ. We stayed in Minnesota, and from the time I was 12 until the age of 18, I attended a Bible-preaching church. I gained a solid Christian foundation that is still with me today. However, my parents and I eventually fell away from the Lord. Both sets of my parents eventually divorced, and we returned to my roots.

Four days after I turned 18, I married someone who was 11 years older than me. We had met at a Baptist church, and we were literally brought together through mutual grief over the death of his young sister—one of my best friends. Eighteen months after we married, we had a daughter. I have always been a strong-willed person and would not allow him to be the leader of our home.

After we divorced, I began living a very non-Christian life. I drank, smoked, lived immorally, and as a result, became very depressed. My attitude was one of utter defeat. I decided that if I was not going to live a Christian life, then I would live totally the opposite. With very little self-esteem, I didn't feel worthy of a good Christian husband. I dated anyone, and that destructive behavior led to my being sexually assaulted. Though I was not physically hurt, I was destroyed mentally. I did not go to the police because I reasoned that I was dating the person, so I deserved what happened. This one act of violence affected my future as it is today.

Eventually, I remarried and had another daughter. While my second husband and I were married, we both were unfaithful. We divorced, and the day after my divorce was final, I married an alcoholic who was very abusive. Throughout our volatile marriage, we divorced, remarried, and finally moved to the "ends of the earth" where we knew no one.

My older daughter wanted to attend church in the small town we chose to make our home. I had seen a church on a main road, made a couple of calls, and Jane (not her real name) started attending that church as a bus kid. She began to make some changes in her life and began attending the church's Christian school.

My husband and I still led our depressing and abusive lives until one night when he decided that life would be better for him if I were not alive. He pulled a gun on me, and when he left the room, I called "9-1-1." I left the house to hide until the police came and took him away.

I decided that perhaps God was trying to tell me something. I had always felt that I deserved whatever happened to me because I was not living right. Even though I was done with my marriage, I wanted to make some changes and began attending church with my daughter.

However, after church I continued visiting the local bar. For any of you who have tried to live two lives, you know that this way of life doesn't work for long. I finally made a choice to try to do the right thing. I was happier, and my life was going on. I hadn't seen my husband since he had been taken to jail, and I was filing for divorce.

Then, to my horror, he was saved while he was in jail. Yes, you read it correctly—I was literally horrified because I thought life was finally great. I knew the right thing to do was to stay married and make things work. I took him back when he was released from jail. He began to attend church also, and we began slowly to rebuild our marriage.

For a few months life was great. We still had some problems but no abuse. About seven months after we were back together, he told me that he no longer wanted to be married to me and he no longer wanted to be a Christian. I told him he could divorce me, but since he had asked Jesus into his heart, he could not ask Jesus to leave. I would later learn that he had been seeing someone else. I truly believe my husband was saved. No one who had led such a wicked life could have made the changes he made in life and **not** be saved. He prayed, read his Bible, and listened to good music.

I moved out as he asked, but I left telling him that I was willing to work things out when he was ready. After much counseling with my pastor, I decided not to fight the divorce. During the time when all of this heartache was happening, I felt like I had been sucker-punched. "How dare You, God, make me go through this when I was trying so hard for the first time in my life!" I thought.

I hated my husband for a time, but I learned the hard way that I must forgive him in order to get on with my life and spiritual walk with God. Ten years after our divorce was final, I finally spoke to my ex-husband at his father's funeral. I tried to encourage him while praying that I could make it through the conversation with grace. Psalm 27:7-28 helped me through this marriage, helped me learn to forgive, and helped me learn the lesson that I am forgiven even though I do not deserve it.

While attending this church, I met and married one of the church members. We then tried to gain the custody of his two children. We were hours away from filing papers to get custody due to neglect when we discovered more than neglect was involved. We received immediate custody of the children. Never in my life had I felt such anger toward another human being. For two years I fumed and became a bitter and unforgiving Christian. Forgiving my ex-husband was easy compared to forgiving those who had hurt my stepchildren. Finally, the Lord showed me I was the one who was wrong, and all of my children were suffering because of my refusal to forgive. I saw that my bitterness was rubbing off on them. I asked my stepchildren to forgive me. Since this time of resolution, the children and I have grown very close, and we work together on forgiving and not being bitter. Both of them want to live for the Lord and to help others who have suffered as they have.

For me, life continues on. Looking back over my life, I can see where poor decisions led me and where the right decisions are leading me now. I would encourage ladies with immorality in their past to make some decisions today.

Decide to Forgive.

Until you forgive all the hurts of your past and those who hurt you, you will be a conduit for bitterness, anger, and poor choices to those around you. Not only will your spirit ache, but so will your family's.

Decide Not to Ride the Fence.

Your life will only begin to turn around when you decide to give it all to God. Just as Jesus gave Himself totally for **you**, it may be time to give yourself totally to **Him**. Following Christ part-time will lead to part-time troubles and tears.

Decide to Fight Negative Influences in Your Life With God's Word.

Cling to God's Word for every situation that arises in your life. Focus on TRUTH rather than FEELINGS. The following verses helped me in areas where I personally struggled.

WHEN I AM FEARFUL:

Psalm 56:3   *"What time I am afraid, I will trust in thee."*

Psalm 56:11   *"In God have I put my trust: I will not be afraid what man can do unto me."*

Psalm 63:2, 3, 7   *"To see thy power and thy glory, so as I have seen thee in the sanctuary. Because thy lovingkindness is better than life, my lips shall praise thee. Because thou hast been my help, therefore in the shadow of thy wings will I rejoice."*

Proverbs 3:24-26   *"When thou liest down, thou shalt not be afraid: yea, thou shalt lie down, and thy sleep shall be sweet. Be not afraid of sudden fear, neither of the desolation of the wicked, when it cometh. For the LORD shall be thy confidence, and shall keep thy foot from being taken."*

WHEN I AM HAVING A PITY PARTY:

Psalm 126:5, 6   *"They that sow in tears shall reap in joy. He that goeth forth and weepeth, bearing precious seed, shall doubtless come again with rejoicing, bringing his sheaves with him."*

Romans 8:18, 28   *"For I reckon that the sufferings of this present time are not worthy to be compared with the glory which shall be revealed in us. And we know that all things work together for good to them that love God, to them who are the called according to his purpose."*

WHEN I AM BITTER:

Romans 12:21   *"Be not overcome of evil, but overcome evil with good."*

When I Need Comfort:

Ephesians 5:19 *"Speaking to yourselves in psalms and hymns and spiritual songs, singing and making melody in your heart to the Lord."*

Philippians 4:11, 13 *"Not that I speak in respect of want: for I have learned, in whatsoever state I am, therewith to be content. I can do all things through Christ which strengtheneth me."*

Decide to Help Others.

You may tend to spend much of your time looking inward rather than upward. Hurts will fade away when you begin to look *outward*. Encourage others who are going through a hard time. Spend time in prayer for a trial someone is going through. Be ready to share what God has done in and with your life. Be a shining example of God's grace.

Decide That God Is Not Finished With You Yet.

Never, ever entertain the thought that you are shelved or unusable to God. He loves and cares for you. In His mercy He has designed a special place in His work, just for YOU. There are people only YOU can reach. There are situations only YOU can totally understand. The Devil only gains victory if you quit and decide to put yourself on the shelf. Remember, hold your head high. YOU are a daughter of the King.

Afterword

L ife is filled with heartaches and fears like those discussed in this booklet. Faith tells us that there is a real place without any sadness or grief—Heaven. Each of the authors in this booklet has a personal testimony of a home in Heaven someday. You too can know 100% for sure, without a doubt, that you can go to Heaven. You need to know the following:

- **Realize there is none good.** Romans 3:10 says, *"As it is written, There is none righteous, no, not one."*

- **See yourself as a sinner.** Romans 3:23 says, *"For all have sinned, and come short of the glory of God."*

- **Recognize where sin came from.** Romans 5:12 says, *"Wherefore, as by one man sin entered into the world, and death by sin; and so death passed upon all men, for that all have sinned."*

- **Notice God's price on sin.** Romans 6:23 says, *"For the wages of sin is death; but the gift of God is eternal life through Jesus Christ our Lord."*

- **Realize that Christ died for you.** Romans 5:8 says, *"But God commendeth his love toward us, in that, while we were yet sinners, Christ died for us."*

- **Take God at His Word.** Romans 10:13 says, *"For whosoever shall call upon the name of the Lord shall be saved."*

- **Claim God's promise for your salvation.** Romans 10:9-11 says, *"That if thou shalt confess with thy mouth the Lord Jesus,* *and shalt believe in thine heart that God hath raised him from the dead, thou shalt be saved. For with the heart man believeth unto righteousness; and with the mouth confession is made unto salvation. For the scripture saith, Whosoever believeth on him shall not be ashamed."*

Now pray. Confess that you are a sinner. Ask God to save you and receive Christ as your personal Saviour.